writing & printing

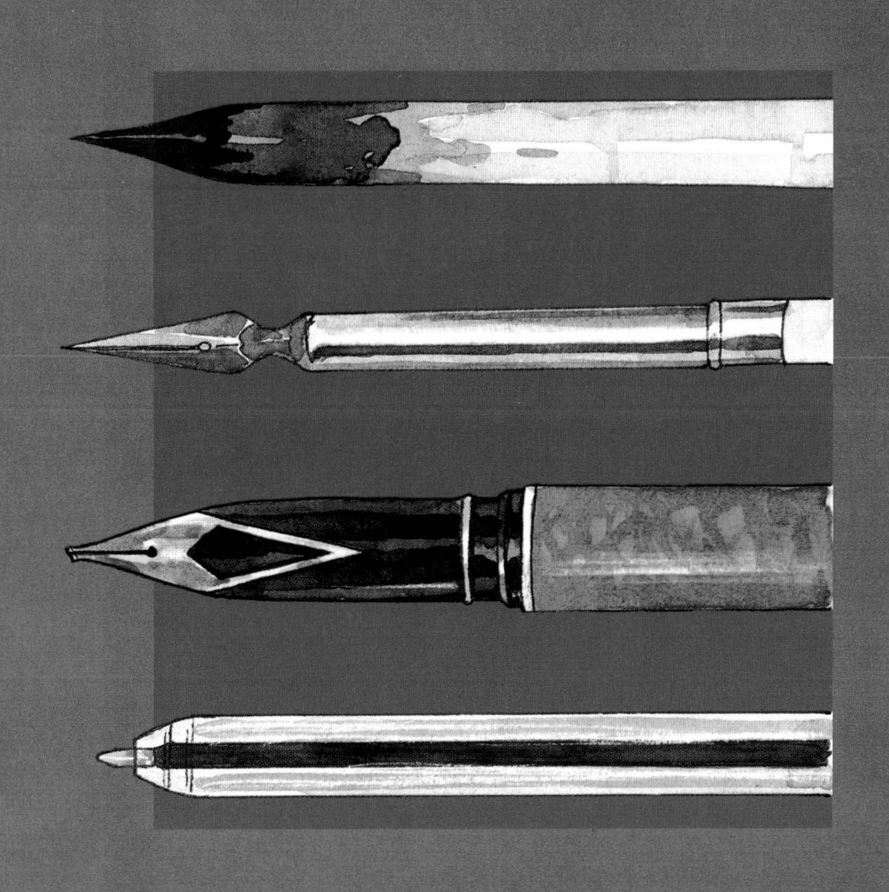

SERIES EDITOR DAVID SALARIYA
BOOK EDITOR APRIL McCROSKIE

First American Edition 1997 by
Franklin Watts
A Division of Grolier Publishing
Sherman Turnpike
Danbury, CT 06816

Library of Congress Cataloging-in-Publication Data

Steedman, Scott.
Writing & Printing / written by Scott Steedman : illustrated by David Antram.
p. cm. – (Worldwise)
Includes index.
Summary: Presents a history of the written word, from hieroglyphics to the printing press to computers.
ISBN 0-531-14424-0 (lib. bdg.). ISBN 0-531-15311-8 (pbk.)
1. Writing – History – Juvenile literature. 2. Printing – History –Juvenile literature. [1. Writing – History. 2. Printing – History.]
I. Antram, David. 1958– ill. II. Title. III. Series.
Z40.S79 1997 96–16051
652.09 – dc20 CIP AC

Printed in Belgium

writing & printing

Written by
SCOTT STEEDMAN
Illustrated by
DAVID ANTRAM
Series Created & Designed by
DAVID SALARIYA

FRANKLIN WATTS
A Division of Grolier Publishing
LONDON • NEW YORK • HONG KONG • SYDNEY
DANBURY, CONNECTICUT

CONTENTS

Why write things down?

Because no one can remember everything. We know that every time a story is told, the details change. And two people who saw the same event might remember it differently. But if it is written down, the story cannot change. People can read your words, even hundreds of years after you die.

The invention of printing was a great step forward. For the first time, ordinary people could afford to read – or even write – their own books. Learning spread far and wide.

Many letters began as pictures. The ancient Egyptians drew an ox head to represent the letter "A."

By 1000 B.C. the picture had become a symbol, aleph, *which means "ox." The Greeks called it* alpha, *the first letter of their alphabet.*

The Romans developed the small letter "a" about 1,700 years ago. Today, we use a similar shape for writing in English.

The first written signs were pictures of everyday objects. But realistic pictures take time to draw. With use, they became simplified and more like symbols. To show complicated ideas like "hunger" or "slowly," writers invented other symbols.

Later, new signs were developed to represent sounds in a language. These signs – called letters – could be strung together to spell words. A set of letters is called an alphabet. Today more people write with alphabets than with any other system.

Prehistoric people painted animals and people on cave walls. These may tell stories of hunting trips.

Greek legend says that the *Iliad* and the *Odyssey* were written by a blind poet, Homer. These poems may have been retold by storytellers who added new details. Finally they were written down.

All Western languages use the Roman alphabet. The many thousands of words in the English language can be written with just 26 letters.

Before writing, tribes had storytellers who recounted myths and legends, often at feasts or other gatherings.

Monk

Before printing was invented, all books had to be copied out by hand. In the Middle Ages, many monks spent their whole lives copying manuscripts. Their beautiful works were rare and very valuable.

Professional writer

This Viking memorial stone is carved with letters called runes.

For years, many people could not read or write. They hired professional writers to write important documents.

The Babylonians and Assyrians both adapted cuneiform. These tablets all contain the word "orchard."

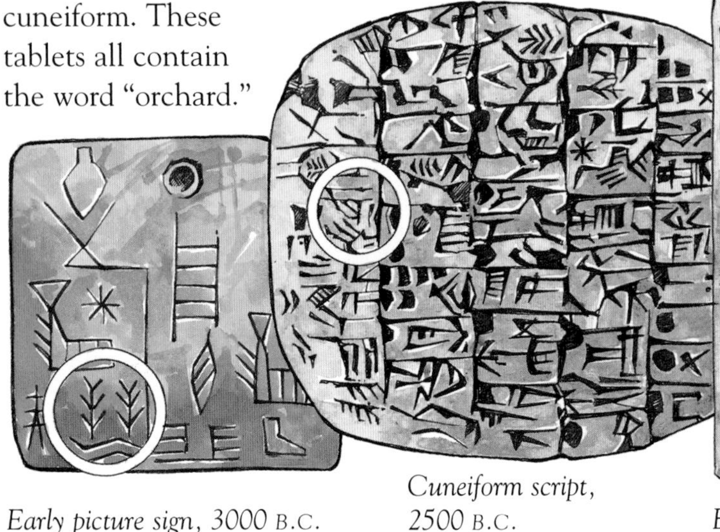

Early picture sign, 3000 B.C.

Cuneiform script, 2500 B.C.

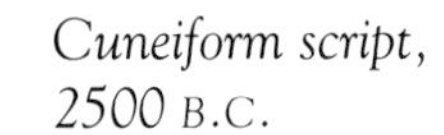

Early Babylonian, 1750 B.C.

Assyrian, 683 B.C.

Sumerian picture sign for the word "orchard."

Scribes began to write sideways on tablets.

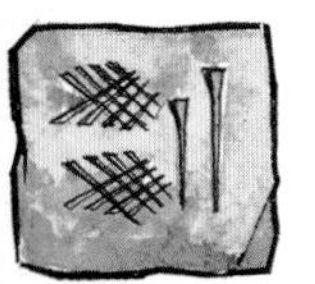

Early Babylonian sign for "orchard."

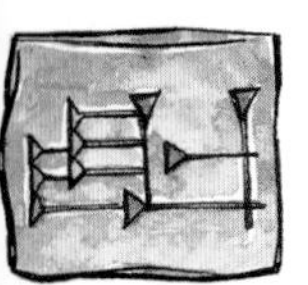

Assyrian sign for "orchard," written with blunt stylus.

The first written language was developed by the Sumerian people of Mesopotamia. By 3000 B.C. they were using reed tools to scratch picture signs into clay. Over the centuries, the signs were simplified until they became groups of wedge-shaped marks. We now call the script "cuneiform," which means "wedge-shaped" in Latin.

Young Babylonian boys were trained to be scribes – professional writers. In addition to reading and writing, they learned math and literature. Scribes worked as record keepers for the government.

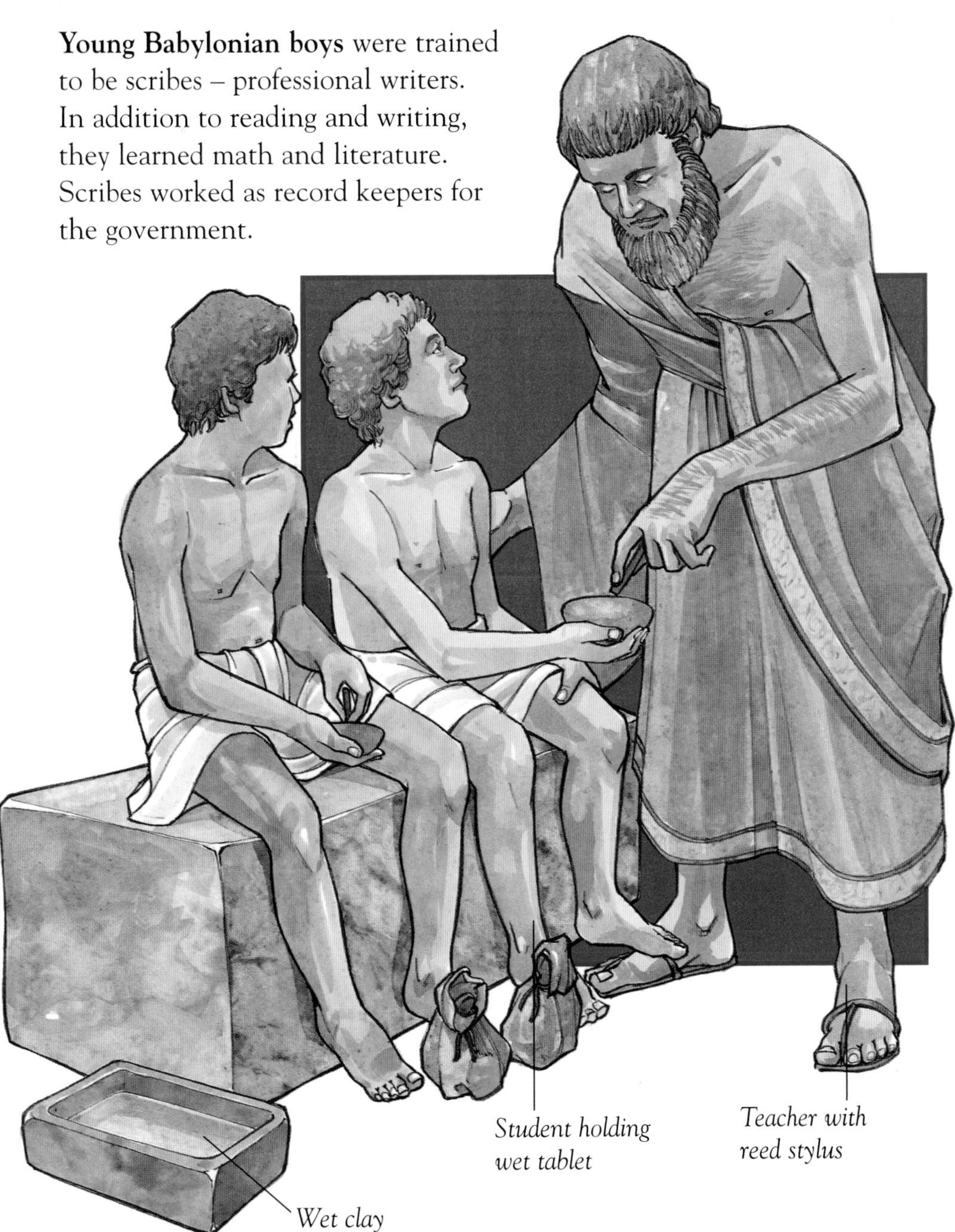

Student holding wet tablet

Teacher with reed stylus

Wet clay

North American Indians painted beautiful pictograms to tell stories of great hunts, battles, or voyages. You do not need to speak their language to be able to "read" the pictograms.

This pictogram shows a figure wearing a striped blanket. Blankets were often traded, so perhaps this pictogram represents a trading expedition.

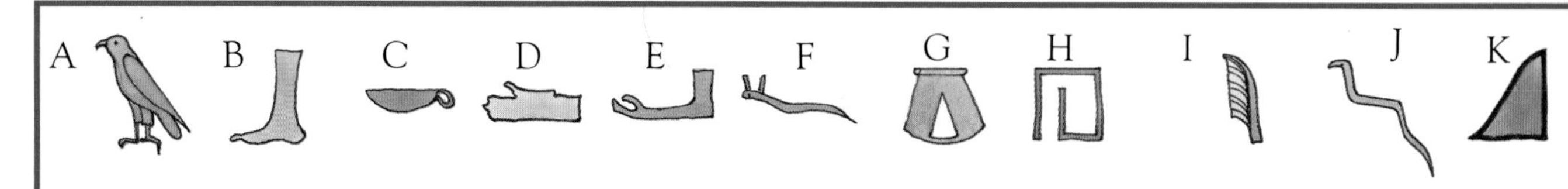

Each hieroglyph in the ancient Egyptian alphabet represented one sound. Words could be spelled out or represented by a drawing.

At the yearly cattle count, an Egyptian farmer led his herd past a scribe, who wrote down all the details. Later the scribe worked out how much tax the farmer owed.

Scribes were the only people who could read or write so they were important in ancient Egyptian society. They sat cross-legged and wrote on scrolls.

This hieroglyph shows a scribe's brush, ink, and palette. If a man was drawn next to it, it meant "scribe." But next to a roll of papyrus paper, it meant "writing."

Palette to hold reed pens.

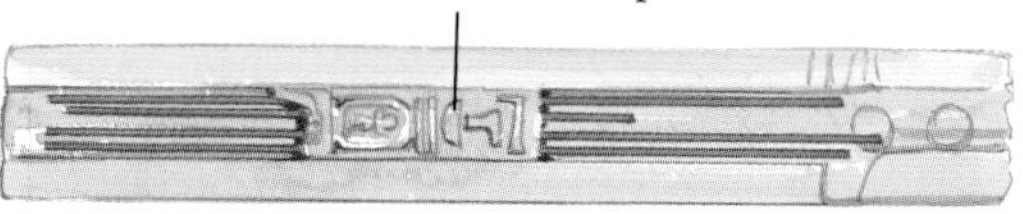

Here are 21 letters of a Roman alphabet, taken from sculptures dating from A.D. 150 to 300.

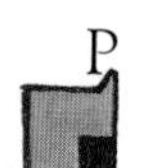

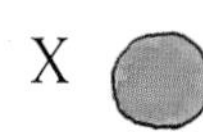

The Egyptians developed a kind of picture-writing about 5,000 years ago. We now call it "hieroglyphs," from two Greek words meaning "sacred carvings." Thousands of hieroglyphs have been decoded. Some are pictures that stand for words like "owl" or "sun." Others represent ideas, like "life," or sounds, like the letters of an alphabet.

The ancient Greeks had a much simpler system, a proper alphabet with only 24 letters. The Romans adapted this alphabet and changed several letters.

The word alphabet comes from *alpha* and *beta*, the first two letters in the Greek alphabet.

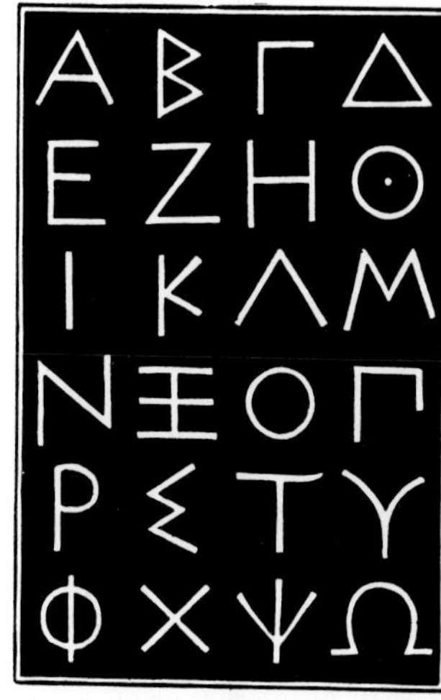

Ancient Greek letters from a stone pillar.

The way of writing the letters of the Roman alphabet has barely changed over the last 2,000 years.

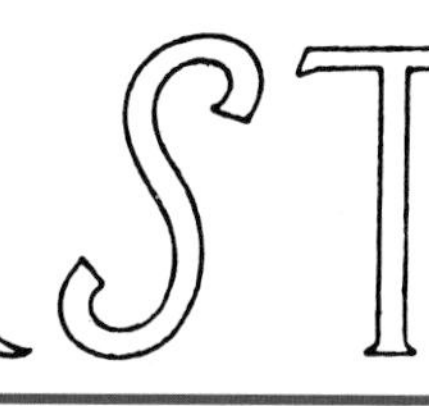

Clay tablet

Clay tablets were easy to make and fit into the palm of the hand. But they were heavy to carry.

Before paper, people wrote on all kinds of materials. The Sumerians used clay tablets, and the Egyptians wrote on stone, wood, and a papery substance called papyrus. In the Middle Ages, monks wrote on parchment, made from animal skins.

Paper was invented by the Chinese around A.D. 105. They kept it a secret until 751, when an Arab army captured some Chinese papermakers.

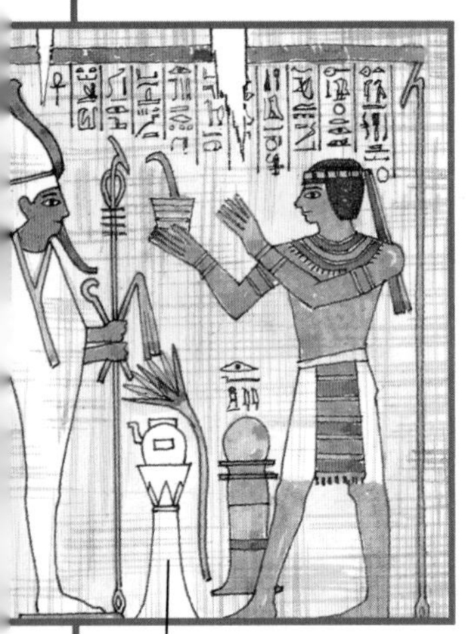

Papyrus was made from the papyrus plant's pulp. This was pounded into strips, then knitted together and dried in the sun. This papyrus is decorated.

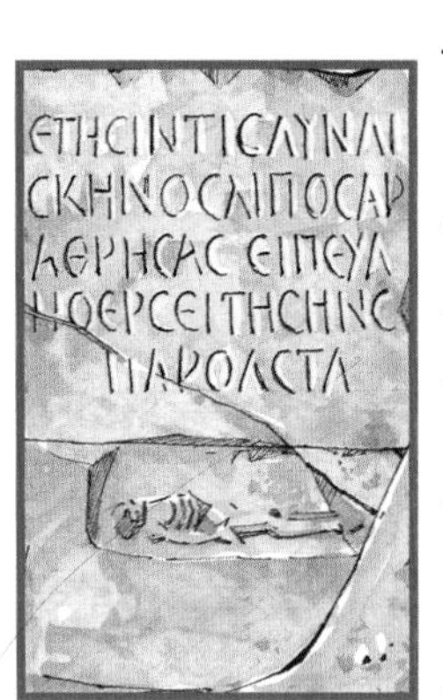

The writing on the Roman tombstone (*left*) is in Latin. Underneath there is a carving of a grinning skeleton.

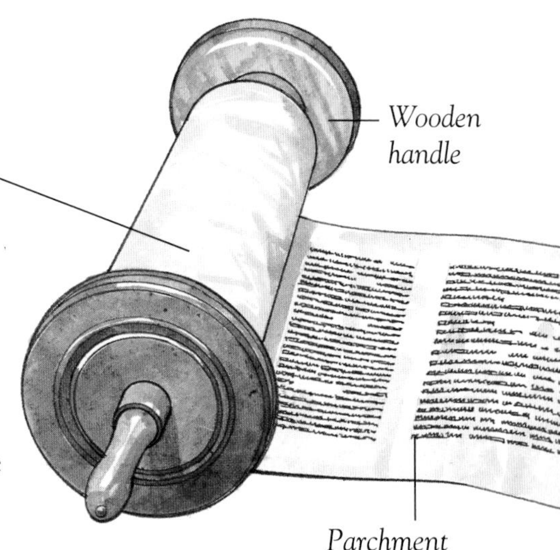

This scroll is the Jewish holy book, the Torah.

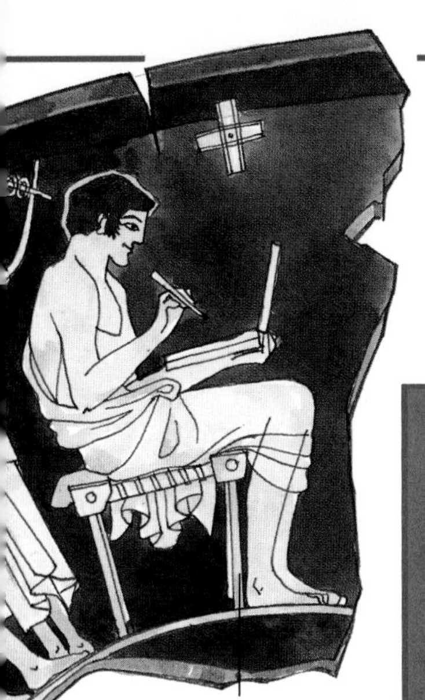

The Greeks and Romans wrote on wax tablets. The metal stylus had a sharp point. The other end was flat, to scrape off work and reuse the tablet.

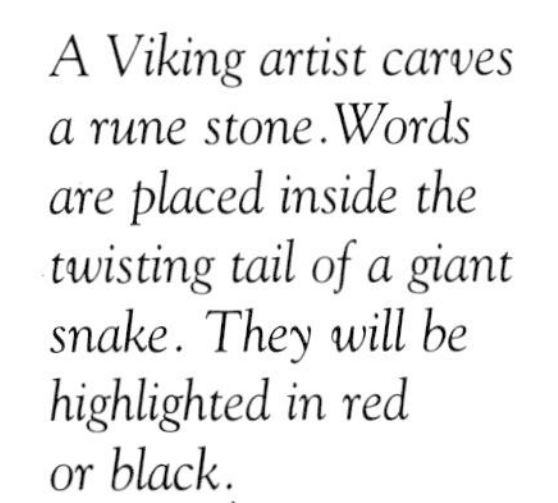

A Viking artist carves a rune stone. Words are placed inside the twisting tail of a giant snake. They will be highlighted in red or black.

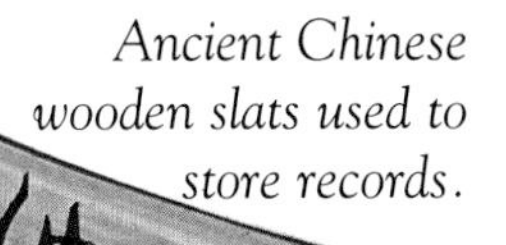

Ancient Chinese wooden slats used to store records.

The Maya of Central America had two writing styles – one for wood or bark, the other for stone or jade.

Animal hide is stretched on a frame to make parchment.

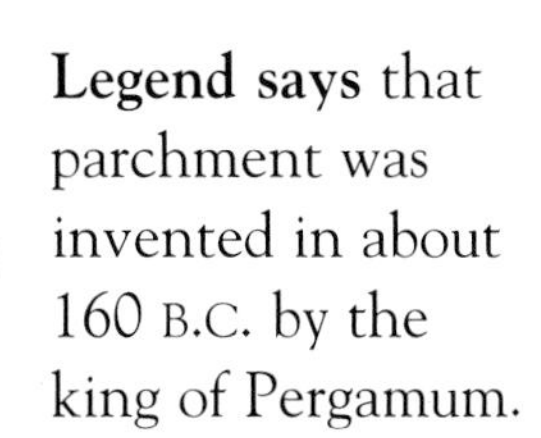

Legend says that parchment was invented in about 160 B.C. by the king of Pergamum.

The ancient Chinese made paper from mulberry leaves or rags. A bamboo mold was used. The water was squeezed out and the paper was left to dry.

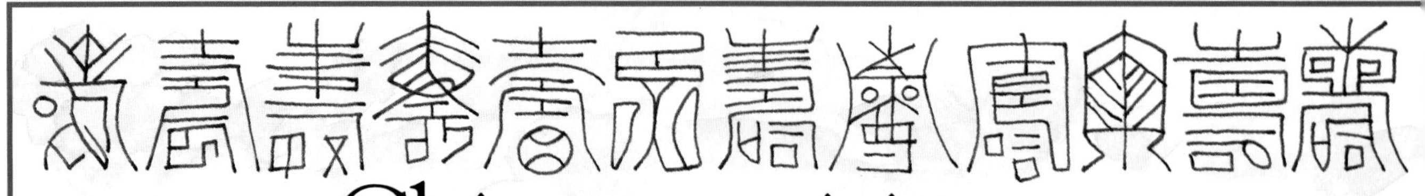

Calligraphy is the art of beautiful writing. Chinese calligraphers spend years perfecting their style. Here are 12 ways of writing the character Shou, *meaning "long life."*

Chinese writing is the oldest system still in everyday use.

It has hardly changed since it was developed 4,000 years ago, so modern Chinese people can read ancient texts. Chinese is based on picture writing. Common words, like "home" or "fire,"are picture signs. Other words are built up from sounds. There are over 50,000 characters (signs) and you need to know about 2,000 to read the newspaper!

Cang Jie

Characters are written with animal-hair brushes. Characters can be made up of more than 20 brush strokes.

Legend says that Chinese writing was invented by Cang Jie. He copied the tracks of animals and birds.

This is the correct way to write "tree."

The earliest known printed book is a Chinese translation of a Buddhist text, called the *Diamond Sutra.* It was printed with carved wood blocks in A.D. 868.

Like Chinese, Japanese is traditionally written in vertical columns and read from right to left.

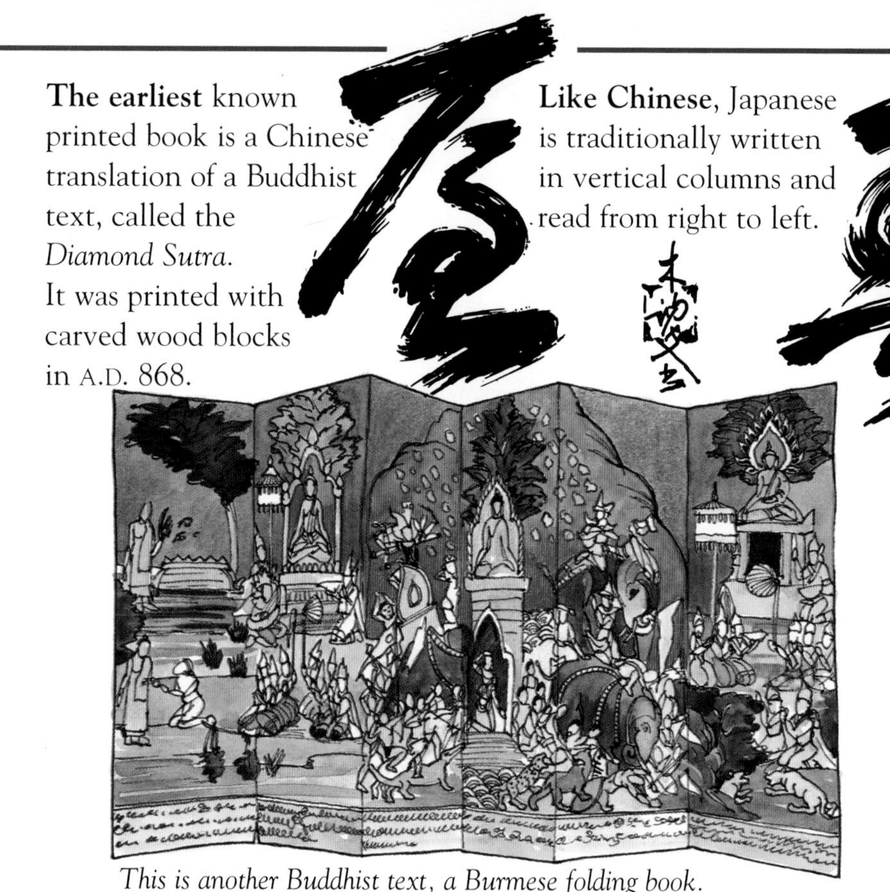

This is another Buddhist text, a Burmese folding book.

There are more than 200 languages in India, and almost as many ways of writing each one. Hindi is usually written in the Devangari alphabet, and Urdu is usually written in Arabic.

This book from Kashmir, India, is in Sarada script.

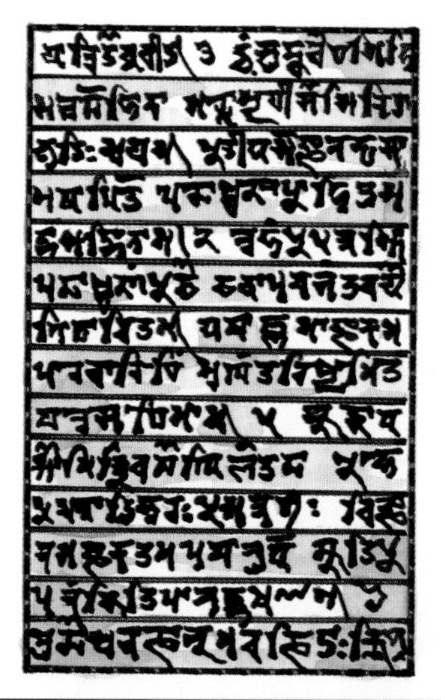

About 1,500 years ago, Japan and Korea used Chinese characters for writing. Japanese still uses many Chinese characters. But in Korean, they were replaced by an alphabet invented by King Sejong in 1443.

Arabic is written in many beautiful scripts. Some are used mainly for religious writings or private letters. Others are popular only in one area.

Arabic is a language spoken by more than 120 million people. It is also an alphabet used to write other languages, like Persian, spoken in Iran and Afghanistan, and Urdu, spoken in India and Pakistan. The alphabet was invented 1,300 years ago, to write down the words of Allah (God), as revealed to the prophet Muhammad. Ever since, Muslims across the world have read

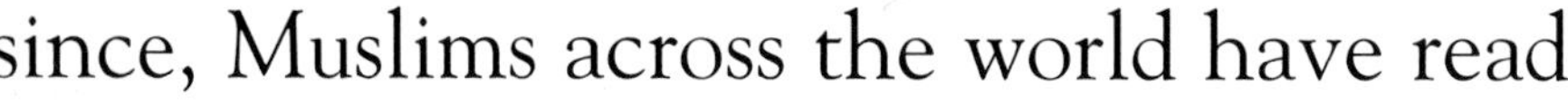

the Koran, the Islamic holy book, in Arabic. In English, we use Arabic numbers.

Islamic scribe, with tools.

The Islamic scribe devotes his life to writing beautiful versions of the Koran.

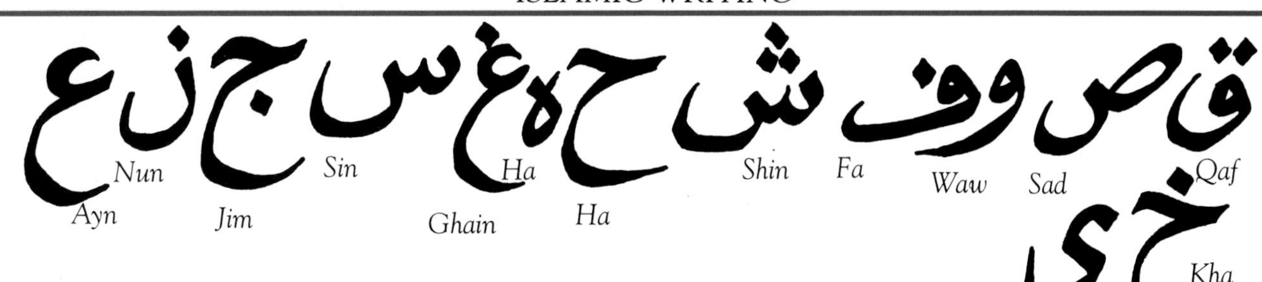

These letters are written separately. When joined, the letters change shape depending on where they are in a word.

Royal Diwani script

Like Chinese, Arabic is read from right to left. Unlike Chinese, it is a true alphabet, with only 29 letters.

Muslims believe that writing is a gift from Allah. Buildings, clothes, pots, even tombstones, are decorated with beautiful holy words.

Diwani script

In Islamic art, realistic pictures are forbidden. So mosques – Muslim holy buildings – are decorated with abstract designs. These include sayings from the Koran.

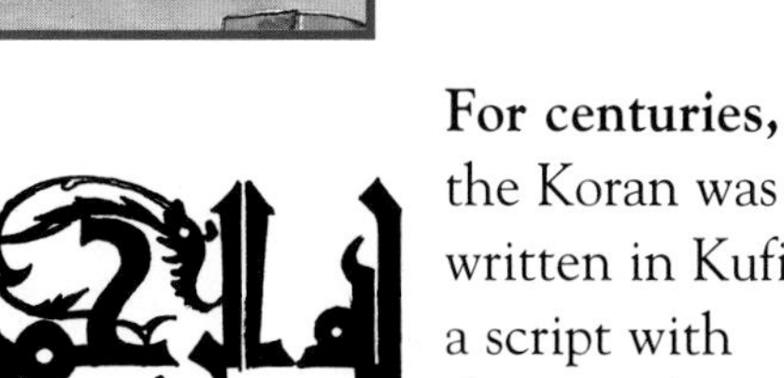

Kufic script

For centuries, the Koran was written in Kufic, a script with sharp angles. Nowadays the Koran is usually written in Nashki, a more rounded script.

This Anglo-Saxon alphabet dates from the early Middle Ages, nearly a thousand years ago. It has 24 letters, two less than today's alphabet.

Writing and book-making in medieval Europe was dominated by the Christian Church. Before printing, all books had to be copied out by hand. Monks dedicated their lives to making Bibles and prayer books. We call them illuminated manuscripts, because they glow with silver and gold decoration.

This "A" is from a manuscript made in England between 1120 and 1140. Notice the animals, people and the knight with his sword.

The monk divided his page into blocks of text with gridlines. He copied out the text, then filled in the leftover space with the large capital letter.

Monks could spend 20 to 30 years writing one book. To fight the boredom, they often added little poems or drawings.

Intricate pictures were often drawn inside the large capital letters. The first letter of each chapter could be a fine work of art.

This book belonged to the English monk Saint Boniface, who died in A.D. 754. Legend says that it was slashed when non-believers tried to murder him.

Church services were conducted in Latin, so the monks read and wrote in Latin, too.

abcdefghiklmn

To print, Gutenberg had to design a typeface – a set of letters that would look good together in any order. He came up with Gothic, or German, script.

Gutenberg was born in Germany around 1400. He may have started printing around 1439. By 1450 he set up a workshop. His first book – probably the first book printed in Europe – was the Mazarin Bible.

Printing is a great invention that changed history. A method using wooden blocks was invented in China in the 800s. A similar method, using metal type, was perfected in Europe by Johann Gutenberg around 1440. The letters, made of lead, were lined up to form blocks of text. These were then covered in ink and pushed against a sheet of paper in a machine called a press. The letters could be washed and reused.

A press could print thousands of pages a day. For the first time, ordinary people could buy books, and learn to read and write.

opqrꝛsſtuvxyz

The first step in printing was typesetting. The typesetter made up the text with metal type. Then the finished page was screwed into a wooden frame. At the press, the text is inked up and printed.

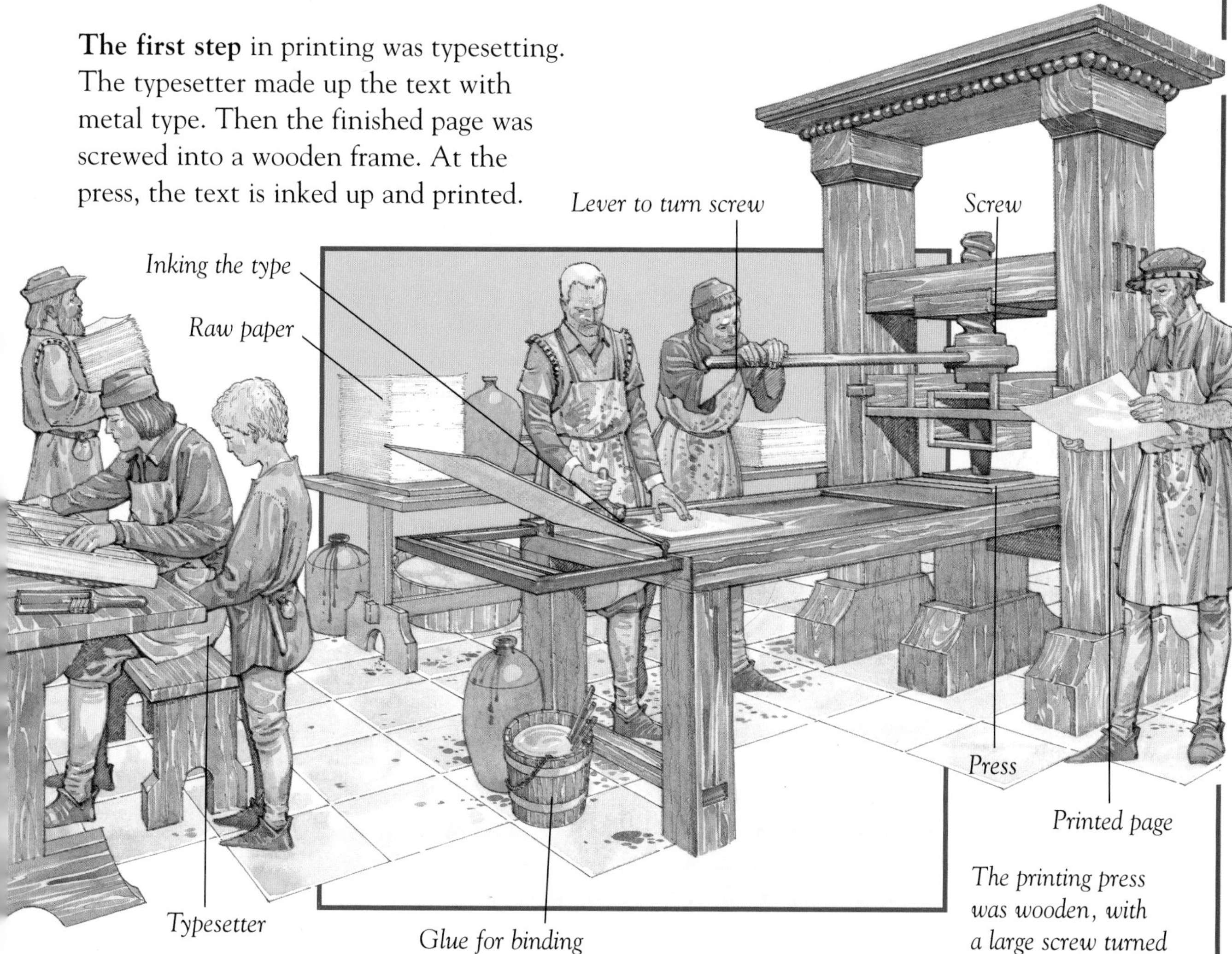

Lever to turn screw

Screw

Inking the type

Raw paper

Press

Printed page

Typesetter

Glue for binding pages together

The printing press was wooden, with a large screw turned by a lever.

ABCDEFGHIJKLMN

Letters come in three forms – lower case, capitals, and small capitals. With numbers and punctuation, a typeface has about 150 characters.

A typeface is a set of letters of the alphabet, including odd characters and spaces, plus punctuation marks, like commas. Before printing, the characters are put together to form pages of text. This job is called typesetting.

Until recently the letters were made of metal. The text was set letter by letter, to form many rows of type, all of the same width. Then the finished page was screwed into a metal frame and inked up for printing.

A piece of type is made by pouring hot metal into a mold. One mold is used to make many copies of the same letter.

Rows of type are created in a tool called a composing stick. The text is upside-down and back-to-front.

The rows are stacked up in a frame called the galley. This is the same size as the page to be printed.

OPQRSTUVWXYZ &

Only the raised part of the block will be printed.

Some letters, like "b" and "y," reach over or under the line of type. The typeface is designed so that they do not touch the lines above or below.

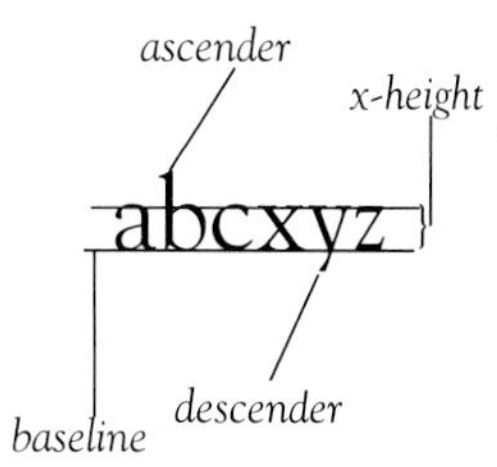

567!+*%Wjh@
Examples of different characters in a typeface.

Each typeface has its own look. Some are easy to read in books; others look best in huge type on posters.

This is Helvetica typeface

This is Bodoni typeface

This is Times typeface

Type size is measured in units called points. This text is 12 point and the big heading is 38 point.

S 65 point

S 52 point

S 43 point

S 36 point

S 28 point

S 16 point

S 14 point

Scripts like this one, which lean forward, are called italic (from the word Italian). Writing them down takes a long time. Some examples of old alphabets do not include the letter 'j'. Often the 'j' was simply an 'i' with an added flourish.

A seal proves who wrote a letter and shows that it has not been opened.

Official document, 1876.

OPQRSTUVWXYZ

Learning to write well takes time. For many years, good handwriting was a sign of a good education. It was also like a personal stamp, as individual as a fingerprint. Before telephones and fax machines, people spread news or ran their businesses by writing letters. Their handwriting and signature guaranteed that a letter was not a fake.

For centuries people wrote with quills – pens made from birds' feathers. The steel-nib pen was invented in 1803.

Quill

Steel-nib pen

Fountain pen

Ballpoint pen

Shorthand was used as early as 63 B.C. It uses signs and abbreviations for words. A lot of information can be written quickly.

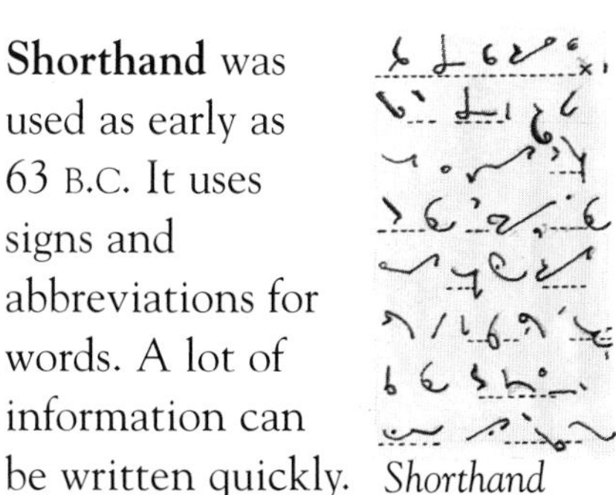

Shorthand

The Remington Company of New York put the first typewriter on sale in 1873. Its QWERTY keyboard is still used on computers.

QWERTY keyboard

The fountain pen was invented in 1884, and Laszlo Biro perfected the ballpoint pen in 1943.

Typewriter print

a b c d e f g h i j k l m n o p q r s t u v w x y z

A newsstand sells newspapers and magazines on nearly every subject you can imagine. Modern printing, even in full color, is quick and fairly cheap. People with unusual hobbies, like quilt making or skydiving, can write about their passions and share them with others. Information, pictures, opinions, and works of art are available to everyone like never before.

New technology keeps improving printing methods. Satellites, fax machines, and computer networks allow news agencies to send stories quickly around the world. Some newspapers are even printed by satellite, producing different editions in different countries, all at the same time!

Newspapers and magazines come in many formats, styles, and languages.

People should be able to read or write whatever they want. But some governments and big companies often try to ban stories which could cause them embarassment. This is called censorship.

If you look closely at a computer screen, you will see that the images are made of thousands of tiny dots. These are called pixels.

Computers can do everything that typewriters, filing cabinets, and typesetters used to do. Instead of typing out every word of every letter, secretaries open a standard letter on the computer screen. They change a few details, then click a button to print it out. Most books, magazines, and newspapers are produced by desktop publishing. The text and pictures are moved into place onscreen. Then the file is sent by cable to the printer, who may be in the next room, or the next continent!

Computers create letters with pixels. Up close, you can see the square edges of every pixel. From a distance, the line appears to be smooth.

Fax is short for facsimile, or exact copy. A fax machine copies a page of text or pictures and sends it to another machine, which prints the page. A good machine takes less than 30 seconds to send a page anywhere in the world.

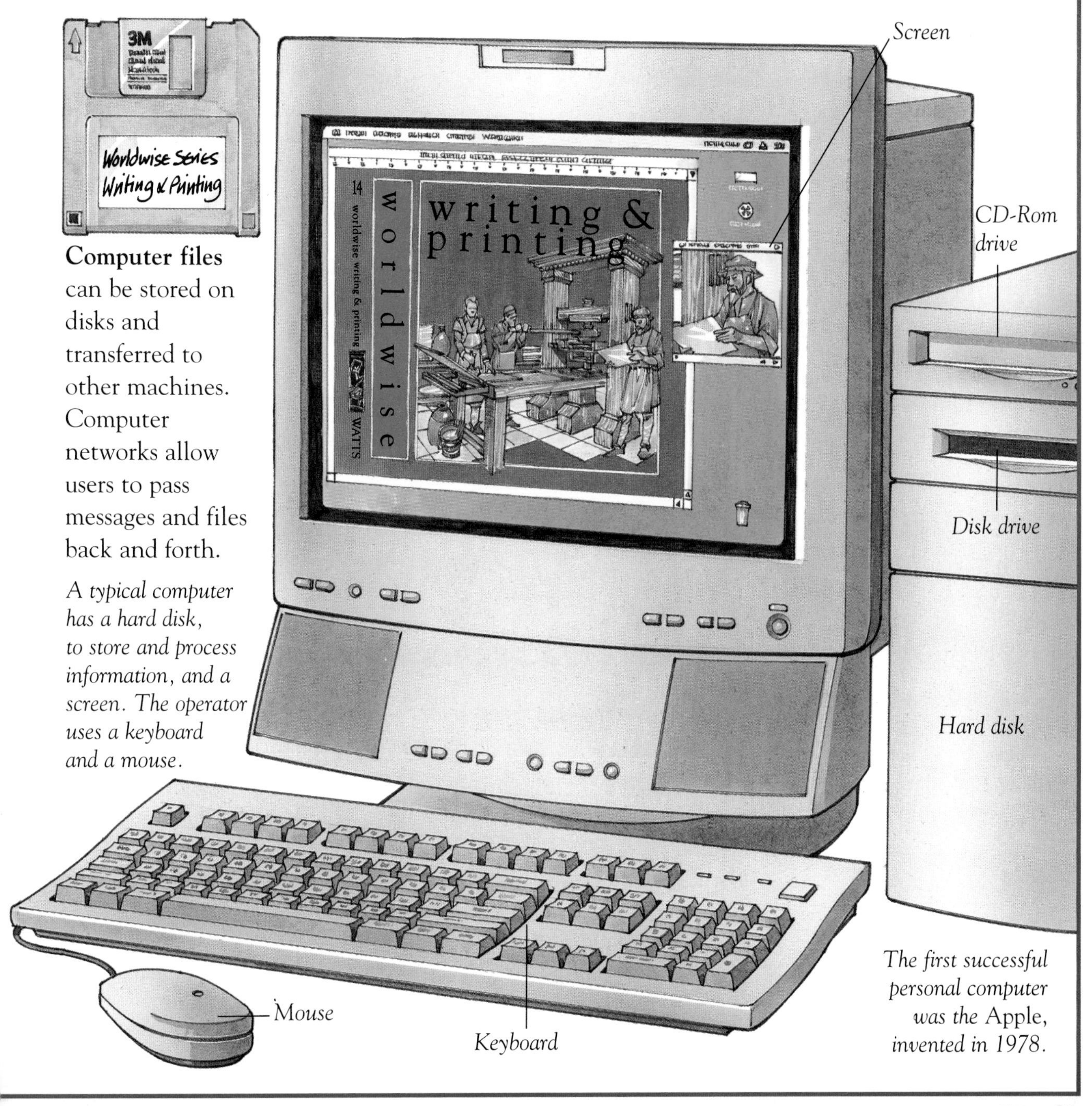

Computer files can be stored on disks and transferred to other machines. Computer networks allow users to pass messages and files back and forth.

A typical computer has a hard disk, to store and process information, and a screen. The operator uses a keyboard and a mouse.

The first successful personal computer was the Apple, invented in 1978.

The Rosetta Stone has text repeated in three languages – Greek, hieroglyphs, and hieratic. Experts who could read Greek used it to understand hieroglyphs.

Jacques-Joseph Champollion was a language expert who helped work out hieroglyphs.

Over the centuries, people have invented hundreds of ways of writing. Some, like Braille and musical notes, have very special uses. Other languages died with the people who wrote them. For more than 1,500 years, no one could read ancient Egyptian hieroglyphs. This system was finally decoded in the early 1800s. Experts can now read tax notes and love poems written over 4,000 years ago. But other ancient languages are still a mystery to us.

P T O L M I I S

K L I O P A D R A

Here are two Egyptian rulers' names – Ptolemy and Cleopatra – as they appear on the Rosetta Stone. The top line is in hieroglyphs; the bottom line is in ancient Greek.

Linear B script

Crete is an island south of Greece. Three thousand years ago, Cretans wrote in three different scripts. Only one, Linear B, has been decoded.

Phaistos disk

Phaistos disk is a mysterious clay object that was found in Crete. It is about 3,500 years old. The 242 signs on the two faces curve inward in spirals. They are picture signs of things like a bird and a fish. But the text has never been translated.

Braille

A	B	C	D	E	F	G
H	I	J	K	L	M	N
O	P	Q	R	S	T	U
V	W	X	Y	Z		

Braille is a system of raised-point writing that blind people can feel with their fingers. The system was invented by Louis Braille in 1829.

Any piece of music can be written down using a special language of notes. A musician who "reads" music will then be able to play it.

In wartime, codes are used to send messages. During World War II, the British cracked *Enigma*, the German code. This breakthrough saved many lives.

Cracking Enigma

This book is part of the Worldwise series. Every Worldwise book has 40 pages, with bright pictures and large text.

This book started as an idea – the publishers thought, why not do a book about writing and printing? They discussed the idea with the author, who wrote a synopsis – a book plan. The designer took the synopsis and drew rough sketches for every page. The designer gave these to an artist, who drew color pictures. The author wrote the text. Both text and pictures were checked by the editor. The book was almost ready to print.

The publisher hires an author. The author researches the subject and writes a book plan, called a synopsis.

The designer works out what each page will look like. He draws sketches for the pictures, and black lines where the text will go.

This book was created as described here. Many books are also created entirely on computer.

The author writes using a computer and sends the text to the editor on a disk.

The editor reads the text. She checks the spelling and grammar. She might also get an expert to check all the facts. If a paragraph is too long, she cuts out a few words.

The editor and artist of this book live in England. But the author lives in France, and the printer is in Belgium!

The artist draws the pictures with colored pencils, ink, oils, or water-colors. He uses a grid to make sure the pictures will fit the page.

Artist

The text is printed out on shiny paper called bromide. The bromide is stuck into place using the rough paste-up as a guide.

The editor prints out the text. Then she cuts it up and sticks it around photocopies of the pictures. This is called a rough paste-up.

Paste-up artist.

Every color you see can be made by mixing yellow, blue, red, and black. These four colors are printed as tiny dots.

Pictures have to be put on film before they are printed. This is done at an origination house. Pictures are processed by a machine called a scanner. It makes four films – yellow, blue, red, and black. The films are made into printing plates. These are clipped into the printing press, inked up, and the press is loaded with paper. Each sheet is printed in each of the four colors. Once dry, it is folded and bound to make a book.

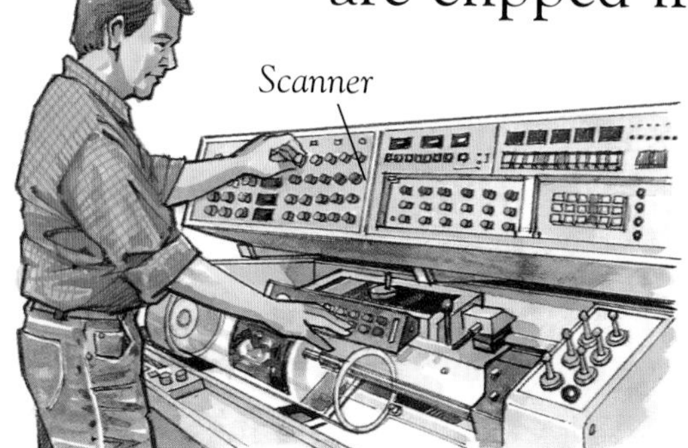

Every picture is separated into its four colors. The scanner measures the amount of yellow, blue, red, and black. Then it works out how many dots of each color are needed.

The people at the origination house use computers to place the pictures on the page. The text is pure black, so it goes on the black film.

Films are placed in the final printing order.

Films are checked before they are sent to the printer.

The films are used to make metal printing plates.

At the origination house

The first sheets are printed on both sides. All 40 pages of the book fit on one sheet of paper.

The plates are wrapped around big rotating drums. There is one drum for each color.

The first printed pages, or "pass sheets" are checked to make sure they match the original drawings.

Thousands of sheets are printed in a few hours. Each one is folded many times into pages. The cover is printed separately, then sewn and glued into place.

The finished books are sent to a warehouse. Bookstores order copies and put them on their shelves. If the book sells well, it will be reprinted.

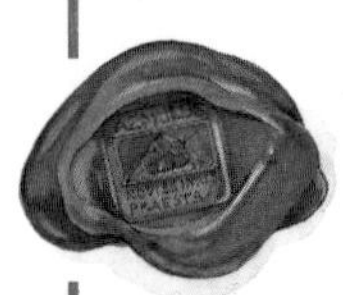

USEFUL WORDS

Alphabet Set of letters used in writing.

Author Writer of a book or article.

Braille System of printing so that blind people can "read" letters with their fingers.

Calligraphy Art of beautiful writing.

Cuneiform The writing of ancient Babylon. The word means "wedge-shaped" in Latin.

Hieroglyphs Ancient Egyptian picture writing. The word means "sacred carving."

Language Speech of one country or group of people, like Chinese or Arabic.

Letter Sign that represents a sound in a language.

Paper Writing material made from wood or rags. Paper was invented in China in about A.D. 105.

Papyrus Papery substance that the ancient Egyptians wrote on. It was made from the papyrus reed.

Parchment Writing material made from animal skins.

Pictogram Symbol that looks like the object it represents.

Press Machine used for printing.

Printing Way of producing books and magazines, using a press.

Runes Viking letters.

Scribe Professional writer.

Typeface Set of letters for printing.

Word Group of letters that can be spoken or written by itself.

INDEX